# Questions and Answers About
# WOMEN'S SUFFRAGE

KATE LIGHT

**PowerKiDS**
press

NEW YO

Published in 2019 by The Rosen Publishing Group, Inc.
29 East 21st Street, New York, NY 10010

First Edition

Editor: Kate Light
Book Design: Michael Flynn

Photo Credits: Cover, p. 7 Bettmann/Getty Images; cover, pp. 1, 3–20, 22–26, 28–32 (background) NuConcept Dezine/Shutterstock.com; p. 5 Library of Congress Rare Book and Special Collections Division; p. 9 Universal History Archive/Universal Images Group/Getty Images; pp. 10, 13 Everett Historical/ Shutterstock.com; p. 11 Epics/Hulton Archive/Getty Images; pp. 15, 23 National Archives and Records Administration; p. 17 Department of Rare Books, Special Collections and Preservation, Rush Rhees Library, University of Rochester; p. 18 Chicago History Museum/Archive Photos/Getty Images; pp. 19, 21 courtesy of the Library of Congress; p. 24 Schlesinger Library, Radcliffe Institute, Harvard University/Bridgeman Images; p. 25 https://en.wikipedia.org/wiki/File:Official_program_-_Woman_suffrage_procession_ March_3,_1913_-_crop.jpg; p. 27 Library of Congress Prints and Photographs Administration; p. 29 Hulton Deutsch/Corbis Historical/Getty Images.

Cataloging-in-Publication Data

Names: Light, Kate.
Title: Questions and answers about women's suffrage / Kate Light.
Description: New York : PowerKids Press, 2019. | Series: Eye on historical sources | Includes glossary and index.
Identifiers: LCCN ISBN 9781538341360 (pbk.) | ISBN 9781538341353 (library bound) | ISBN 9781538341384 (6 pack)
Subjects: LCSH: Women–Suffrage–United States–History–Juvenile literature. | Suffragists–United States–Biography–Juvenile literature. | Women–Political activity–United States–Juvenile literature.
Classification: LCC JK1898.L54 2019 | DDC 324.6'230973–dc23

Manufactured in the United States of America

CPSIA Compliance Information: Batch #CS18PK: For Further Information contact Rosen Publishing, New York, New York at 1-800-237-9932

# CONTENTS

# WHAT IS SUFFRAGE?

A democracy is a form of government controlled by the people. Usually, citizens vote for leaders. Suffrage, or the right to vote, is one of the most important rights for citizens in a democracy. Throughout history, democracies have limited which citizens have the right to vote, often **discriminating** based on race, wealth, or **gender**.

Early on in United States history, only white men who owned land were allowed to vote. In 1870, the Fifteenth Amendment protected suffrage for black men. Women's suffrage didn't become national law until 1920. That important victory occurred after years of hard work by suffragists, or people who believed women should be equal to men. This was an enormous step forward in the fight for women's rights that continues today.

## Equal Franchise Society

### Legislative Series

(EXTRACT FROM A LETTER FROM MRS. ABIGAIL ADAMS
TO HER HUSBAND JOHN ADAMS)

*"I long to hear that you have declared our independency. And, by the way, in the new code of laws which I suppose it will be necessary for you to make, I desire you would remember the ladies and be more generous and favorable to them than your ancestors. Do not put such unlimited power into the hands of the husbands. Remember, all men would be tyrants if they could. If particular care and attention is not paid to the ladies, we are determined to foment a rebellion, and will not hold ourselves bound by any laws in which we have no voice or representation.*

*"That your sex are naturally tyrannical is a truth so thoroughly established as to admit of no dispute; but such of you as wish to be happy willingly give up the harsh title of master for the more tender and endearing one of friend. Why, then, not put it out of the power of the vicious and the lawless to use us with cruelty and indignity with impunity?*

*—"Braintree, March 31, 1776"*

THIS FLYER WAS PRINTED BY THE EQUAL FRANCHISE SOCIETY, AN ORGANIZATION THAT SUPPORTED WOMEN'S RIGHTS. IT FEATURES PART OF A LETTER WRITTEN BY ABIGAIL ADAMS.

## Sources from the Past

Abigail Adams's husband, John Adams, was a member of the Second Continental Congress and later became the second president of the United States. Abigail Adams asked her husband to give women equal rights in the new American government. The original letter Abigail Adams wrote is a primary source. This flyer has a copy of the letter, which makes it a secondary source. How can secondary sources help save information from primary sources?

# ABOLITIONIST AND SUFFRAGE MOVEMENTS

Many women who fought for the right to vote were also members of the abolitionist movement. Abolitionists were people who fought to abolish, or end, slavery. They believed black people should be free and have the same rights as white people. Women took on major roles in the movement. They had opportunities to speak and write against slavery and to participate, or take part, in organizations.

Lucretia Mott and Elizabeth Cady Stanton were both abolitionists. They met in 1840 at the World Anti-Slavery **Convention** in London, England. Women were asked to watch the convention, but they weren't allowed to participate. Mott and Stanton were angry that they weren't allowed to participate. They started brainstorming ideas for a convention that would fight for women's rights. This would eventually lead to the Seneca Falls Convention of 1848.

SOMETIMES PEOPLE FOUGHT BACK AGAINST
THE ABOLITIONIST MOVEMENT WITH **VIOLENCE**.
THIS IMAGE SHOWS LUCRETIA MOTT
SURROUNDED BY AN ANGRY PROSLAVERY MOB.

# THE DECLARATION OF SENTIMENTS

In the summer of 1848, Mott and Stanton worked with other **activists** to plan the Seneca Falls Convention. Part of the planning included writing the Declaration of Sentiments, which explained the purpose of the convention.

The Declaration of Sentiments copied the beginning of the Declaration of Independence, but it had one difference. The Declaration of Independence said that "all men are created equal." The Declaration of Sentiments said that "all men and women are created equal." The Declaration of Sentiments also listed 18 grievances, or complaints, to explain how men had more power than women. Women couldn't vote, attend college, own property, or be leaders in most churches. The Declaration of Sentiments also stated that women should have the right to vote. The Seneca Falls Convention was about to begin.

# THE FIRST CONVENTION

EVER CALLED TO DISCUSS THE

## Civil and Political Rights of Women,

SENECA FALLS, N. Y., JULY 19, 20, 1848.

———

### WOMAN'S RIGHTS CONVENTION.

———

A Convention to discuss the social, civil, and religious condition and rights of woman will be held in the Wesleyan Chapel, at Seneca Falls, N. Y., on Wednesday and Thursday, the 19th and 20th of July current; commencing at 10 o'clock A. M. During the first day the meeting will be exclusively for women, who are earnestly invited to attend. The public generally are invited to be present on the second day, when Lucretia Mott, of Philadelphia, and other ladies and gentlemen, will address the Convention.*

———

\* This call was published in the *Seneca County Courier*, July 14, 1848, without any signatures. The movers of this Convention, who drafted the call, the declaration and resolutions were Elizabeth Cady Stanton, Lucretia Mott, Martha C. Wright, Mary Ann McClintock, and Jane C. Hunt.

## Sources from the Past

Mott, Stanton, and other activists advertised the Seneca Falls Convention through newspapers. This pamphlet has a copy of an advertisement that was published in the *Seneca County Courier* newspaper. Do you think the pamphlet is a primary or secondary source? What does this pamphlet tell you about how people communicated in the mid-1800s? How does this look different from advertisements today?

# THE SENECA FALLS CONVENTION

The Seneca Falls Convention was held on July 19 and 20, 1848, in Seneca Falls, New York. Only women were invited to come the first day. Men were welcomed on the second day. On the first day, Elizabeth Cady Stanton read the Declaration of Sentiments. In the afternoon, the Declaration of Resolutions was read. It listed 11 rights that women ought to have. This document encouraged women to fight for equal rights.

FIRST CONVENTION FOR WOMAN'S RIGHTS WAS HELD ON THIS CORNER 1848

STATE EDUCATION DEPARTMENT 1932

THE 1848 CONVENTION WAS HELD IN THE WESLEYAN CHAPEL IN SENECA FALLS, NEW YORK. PEOPLE CAN STILL VISIT THIS HISTORIC SITE TODAY.

Over 300 people came to the convention, including at least 40 men. Frederick Douglass, an abolitionist and former slave, spoke in support of women's right to vote. By the end of the convention, 68 women and 32 men had signed the declaration. Many historians consider this the beginning of the women's suffrage movement.

# THE AMERICAN EQUAL RIGHTS ASSOCIATION

Newspapers around the country wrote about the Seneca Falls Convention. Some praised the convention, while others wrote bad things about it. Suffragists continued to fight for women's rights anyways. In 1866, the American Equal Rights Association (AERA) was founded. AERA fought for universal suffrage. "Universal" meant for everyone, including black men and all women.

In 1867, there was a public vote in Kansas to decide whether to give more people the right to vote. During the campaign, Elizabeth Cady Stanton and Susan B. Anthony worked with a man who was widely known to be **racist**. Many AERA members were against Stanton and Anthony's actions. The group began to argue about the direction of the movement. Unfortunately, white men in Kansas voted against giving suffrage to either women or black men.

FREDERICK DOUGLASS WAS A LEADER IN THE ABOLITIONIST MOVEMENT AND IN THE WOMEN'S SUFFRAGE MOVEMENT.

13

# AMENDING THE CONSTITUTION

The Thirteenth Amendment ended slavery in 1865. The American Civil War ended that same year. Abolitionists wanted to make sure freed slaves had the same rights as white Americans. Suffragists hoped women would gain equal rights at the same time as the freed slaves.

In 1866, Congress passed the Fourteenth Amendment. It protected freed slaves and promised them rights as citizens of the United States. This amendment was also the first time the Constitution used the word "male" to talk about voters. Anthony, Stanton, and many other suffragists were against the amendment because it said only men could vote. The Fifteenth Amendment passed in 1870. It gave black men the right to vote, but not women. Still, many states illegally refused to let black men vote.

# A PETITION

FOR

# UNIVERSAL SUFFRAGE.

- - -

**To the Senate and House of Representatives:**

The undersigned, Women of the United States, respectfully ask an amendment of the Constitution that shall prohibit the several States from disfranchising any of their citizens on the ground of sex.

In making our demand for Suffrage, we would call your attention to the fact that we represent fifteen million people—one half the entire population of the country—intelligent, virtuous, native-born American citizens; and yet stand outside the pale of political recognition.

The Constitution classes us as "free people," and counts us *whole* persons in the basis of representation; and yet are we governed without our consent, compelled to pay taxes without appeal, and punished for violations of law without choice of judge or juror.

The experience of all ages, the Declarations of the Fathers, the Statute Laws of our own day, and the fearful revolution through which we have just passed, all prove the uncertain tenure of life, liberty and property so long as the ballot—the only weapon of self-protection—is not in the hand of every citizen.

Therefore, as you are now amending the Constitution, and, in harmony with advancing civilization, placing new safeguards round the individual rights of four millions of emancipated slaves, we ask that you extend the right of Suffrage to Woman—the only remaining class of disfranchised citizens—and thus fulfil your Constitutional obligation "to Guarantee to every State in the Union a Republican form of Government."

As all partial application of Republican principles must ever breed a complicated legislation as well as a discontented people, we would pray your Honorable Body, in order to simplify the machinery of government and ensure domestic tranquillity, that you legislate hereafter for persons, citizens, tax-payers, and not for class or caste.

For justice and equality your petitioners will ever pray.

| NAMES. | RESIDENCE. |
|---|---|
| Elizabeth Cady Stanton, | New York |
| Susan B. Anthony | Rochester — N.Y. |
| Antoinette Brown Blackwell | New York |
| Lucy Stone | Newark N. Jersey |
| Joanna S. Morse | 48 Livingston. Brooklyn |
| Ernestine L. Rose | New York |
| Harriet E. Eaton | 6, West 14th Street N.Y. |
| Catharine C. Wilkeson | 83 Clinton Place New York |
| Elizabeth R. Tilton | 46 Livingston St. Brooklyn |
| Mary Fowler Gilbert | 295 W. 19" St New York |
| Mary S. Gilbert | New York |
| M. Griffith | New York. |

# THE AERA DIVIDES

Anthony and Stanton were against the Fifteenth Amendment. They didn't want suffrage granted to black men if women weren't also included. They thought this would exclude, or leave out, women even more. Other suffragists, such as Lucy Stone, strongly supported the Fifteenth Amendment. They saw it as an important step toward universal suffrage. The AERA split into two groups over these disagreements in 1869.

Anthony and Stanton founded the National Woman Suffrage Association (NWSA). The NWSA's goal was to gain women's suffrage through an amendment to the U.S. Constitution. This would grant women's suffrage to the whole country at once. Stone founded the American Woman Suffrage Association (AWSA). It fought for universal suffrage and was willing to support suffrage for black men first. The AWSA worked to add amendments to each state's constitution.

# The Revolution.

*THE TRUE REPUBLIC.—MEN, THEIR RIGHTS AND NOTHING MORE: WOMEN, THEIR RIGHTS AND NOTHING LESS.*

VOL. V.—NO. 21.  NEW YORK, THURSDAY, MAY 26, 1870.  WHOLE NO. 125.

## The Revolution.

PUBLISHED WEEKLY, $3 A YEAR.

NEW YORK CITY SUBSCRIBERS, $3.20.

**ELIZABETH CADY STANTON, Editor.**
**PAULINA WRIGHT DAVIS, Cor. Editor.**
**SUSAN B. ANTHONY, Proprietor.**

OFFICE, 27 CHATHAM STREET, N. Y.

### ANNIVERSARY
#### OF THE

NATIONAL WOMAN SUFFRAGE ASSO-
CIATION.

REPORT OF THE EXECUTIVE COMMITTEE, SUBMIT-
TED MAY 10TH, 1870.

On this our first anniversary it may be well
to recall the particulars of the organization of
our Association and inasmuch as some very
incorrect statements have been put forth by
persons who were not present on that very in-
teresting occasion, we ask the friends present
to a strict attention to the report of the actual
facts. On Saturday evening, May 15th, 1869, the
friends of Woman Suffrage met for a reception, by an invitation given in public by Mrs.
Livermore, at the "Woman's Bureau," 49
East 23d street. On that evening after they
assembled in sufficient numbers to fill the parlors, halls and stairways, Miss Anthony announced that at the urgent request of the nu-
merous delegates to the late Equal Rights Association, the reception would assume the char-
acter of a formal meeting. Mrs. Stanton was
then called to the chair and introduced Mrs.
Randall (who was also appointed Secretary
*pro tem.*). Mrs. Randall stated that many of
the delegates and friends of women who had
attended the anniversary of the Equal Rights
Association were dissatisfied with the very small
amount of time allotted to the question of Woman's Suffrage upon its platform, and desired
that some kind of a distinctive Woman's Suffrage Association might be organized before
they left the city for their homes. Many delegates had come with instructions from their
respective societies to urge the formation of such
an organization, and as so many of the friends,
and especially so many of these very delegates,
were present on this occasion, it seemed a most
favorable time for taking the preliminary steps
toward that object.

After these explanatory remarks—confirmed
by the testimony of others present—it was voted
to organize a "*National Woman's Suffrage Association.*" A constitution was prepared and
accepted, and about one hundred persons, both
men and women, registered their names as
members of this new Association. These members were from all parts of the country and ap-
peared eager to join the first "*National Woman's Suffrage Association*" ever organized in

this country. The only object of the Association
was announced to be to secure the passage of a
"Sixteenth Amendment." Mrs. Stanton was
elected President with enthusiastic demonstra-
tions. Mrs. Ernestine L. Rose was made Chair-
man of the Executive Committee. By vote,
the Executive Committee were empowered to
complete the organization and report on the
17th of the same month.

Thus was organized the Association whose
anniversary we celebrate to-day.

It has never been claimed by us that we ar-
rived at perfectness in either the constitution
or the operations of our Association; it was only
designed to carry us more swiftly to the ballot-
box by a concentration of action to a single
point. We never intended to make it infallible
arms by the complication of its machinery,
neither was it sprung into being to outwit *any-
body*, or to serve the personal ambition of indi-
viduals. It was generated by the creative force
of necessity.

During the year the committee have endeavor-
ed to do their work regardless of the hindrances
ever in the way of every reform. They have
held conventions, authorized lectures, organized
societies in states, towns and counties—sent
out tracts and held correspondence with friends
of the cause at home and abroad, and have
done whatever else they could to hasten the
one object of their creation, viz. : a Sixteenth
Amendment to the Federal Constitution, secur-
ing Suffrage to women.

During the summer of 1869, a circular letter
was issued by some well-known advocates of
the ballot for women, asking signatures to
a *Call* for a *National Convention* to be held
for the sole purpose of organizing a "*Truly*"
"National Woman's Suffrage Association."
Mrs. Stanton, our President—received one of
the circular letters, and returned an answer, in
substance, that "We already had such an organization." When this call was issued, the National Association was not invited as an *association* to attend the Convention, and as far as your
committee have been able to ascertain the facts
in the case, after a great deal of careful inquiry,
not one resident of this city who held office in
the *National Association*, received an invitation.
The State Association, being auxiliary to the
National, did not therefore appoint any delegates to that convention. Thus the most important state in the Union was not represented
in the new organization.

Several members of the National Association
who had united in the call not recognizing
any such a convention was to be held in
Cleveland ......................................
to you to-................................
to send the........................................
but we read.....................................
members u.......................................

*To the Committee of the National .......................
man Suffrage Association."*

FRIENDS : We, resident members of the National Woman's Suffrage Association, not fully recognizing the

force of the reasons *publicly* given for the formation
of an "American Suffrage Association" desire to state
to you in this letter, a few particulars connected with
the organization of the National Woman's Suffrage Association.

In reading the statements herein made, we will ask
you to bear in mind, that they are made by women
who, until last May, had never been identified with any
movement for Woman Suffrage.

Those persons, who were present at the last meeting
of the Equal Right's Association, held in Cooper Union,
in May, will recollect that at the close of the meeting,
Mrs. Livermore, from the platform, invited all the
friends of the cause of "Equal Rights" to attend a
reception to be given at the "Woman's Bureau" the
following Saturday evening. On the day after this an-
nouncement, at the meeting of the "Equal Right's Association" in Brooklyn, we were shown a call, prepared
by Mrs. Mary L. Booth for a meeting of women for the
formation of a Woman's Suffrage Association. This
friend, who consulted in regard to the mat-
ter, she declared herself unwilling to be identified with
any new association; and other prominent ladies ex-
pressing the same unwillingness, the call was not published as contemplated.

All day Saturday, delegates to the "Equal Right's
Association" were coming into the "Woman's Bureau,"
requesting and almost demanding that a National Woman's Suffrage Association should at once be organized
as they had come from all parts of the country to represent the cause of woman, and they could serve as delegates in the new association. The desire was unanimous
on the part of these delegates that there should be an
association of some kind, which should be a centre from
which to work during the coming year. The pressure
was too great to be resisted.

Among the persons prominent in urging the formation of such an association were Mrs. Livermore, Mrs.
Doggett, Mrs. Griffing, Miss Booth, Mrs. Rose, and Mrs.
P. W. Davis, women whose intelligent interest in the
cause you will fully appreciate.

Before the hour appointed for the reception, the
parlors, halls and stairways were crowded—from all
these people came the demand for immediate organization.

Among the persons making this demand were representatives from 19 states and territories, viz. : Maine, 3,
Vermont, 1, New Hampshire, 1, Massachusetts, 5, Rhode
Island, 2, Connecticut, 1, New Jersey, 7, Pennsylvania, 3,
Illinois, 3, Ohio, 3, Wisconsin, 1, Minnesota, 1, Missouri,
3, Kansas, 2, Nebraska, 1, California, 5, District Colum-
bia, 3, Washington Territory, 1.

The remainder of the one hundred members, who
joined the association that evening, resided in different
parts of the state of New York.

In compliance with this unanimous desire, the organization was effected. It was decided by vote that the
President should be elected by acclamation ; there was
but one name spoken by the multitude—that of Elizabeth Cady Stanton. Mrs. A. T. Randall was elected
Secretary, *pro. tem.* After the names of the representatives from various parts of the country had been
enrolled, Vice-Presidents and Advisory Counsels were
appointed for each state as far as possible.

Mrs. E. L. Rose, Mrs. P. W. Davis, Mrs. E. R. Phelps,
Miss S. B. Anthony, Mrs. C. B. Wilbour were consti-

the country to express their views upon any subject
bearing upon the question of the ballot for woman.

While we rejoice in any movement which has for [its]

# BLACK WOMEN OF THE SUFFRAGE MOVEMENT

Black women were often left out by white women within the suffragist movement. Meetings and marches organized by white suffragists often **segregated** black women. Many black women started their own clubs and organizations, including the National Association of Colored Women (NACW). The NACW was founded in 1896 by Harriet Tubman, Ida B. Wells, Mary Church Terrell, and other activists. The NACW's goal was to improve the lives of black Americans in many areas, including women's suffrage.

IDA B. WELLS WAS A SUFFRAGIST AND A JOURNALIST WHO WROTE ARTICLES ABOUT RACIAL ISSUES. SHE HELPED FOUND THE NATIONAL ASSOCIATION OF COLORED WOMEN.

Mary Church Terrell, a suffragist, became the NACW's first president. She fought for job training, equal pay, and childcare. The NACW also fought against racial segregation and violence against black Americans. This organization still works to help women and children today. It's now called the National Association of Colored Women's Clubs (NACWC).

Many black activists, such as Ida B. Wells, fought for rights for both black Americans and women. Wells fought against violence, such as **lynching**, through writing and giving speeches. In 1892, she started an antilynching campaign after three of her friends were killed by a white mob. In 1913, Wells founded the Chicago Alpha Suffrage Club. This was likely the first black women's suffrage club.

Sojourner Truth was another important activist. She supported abolition, universal suffrage, and equality for black Americans and women. Truth was a former slave who gained her freedom in 1827. She gave her famous "Ain't I a Woman?" at a women's rights convention in Ohio in 1851. She argued that women and men had equal abilities and should have equal rights.

SOJOURNER TRUTH BEGAN SPEAKING AGAINST SLAVERY IN 1843. SHE WAS ENCOURAGED BY OTHER FEMALE LEADERS, INCLUDING LUCRETIA MOTT, AND SPENT THE REST OF HER LIFE SPEAKING OUT ABOUT WOMEN'S RIGHTS AND UNIVERSAL SUFFRAGE.

21

# THE NEW DEPARTURE

In the 1870s, suffragists tried a new strategy called the New Departure. The Fourteenth Amendment said everyone born in the United States was a citizen. Suffragists argued women were citizens who had the same rights as men, including the right to vote.

In 1872, Susan B. Anthony and a group of women convinced men at the voter **registration** office to let them register using this argument. Two weeks after voting, Anthony was arrested for voting illegally. The judge ruled that the Fourteenth Amendment didn't give women the right to vote. Anthony was found guilty on June 19, 1873.

In 1875, the Supreme Court ruled on Virginia Minor's case. She had tried to vote in 1872, too. The Supreme Court also ruled that women didn't have the right to vote under the Fourteenth Amendment.

COMMITMENT.     Stump & Southworth, Printers, Reynolds' Arcade, Rochester, N.Y.

# Circuit Court of the United States,
## FOR THE NORTHERN DISTRICT OF NEW YORK,
### MONROE COUNTY.

To _Isaac F. Quinby_ , Marshal of the United States, for the Northern District of New York, and his Deputies, or either of them, and to the Keeper of the common Jail of the County of _Albany N Y_

These are to Command you, The said Marshal and Deputies, or either of you, to convey and deliver into the custody of the said keeper, the body of _Susan B. Anthony_ charged this day before me, a Commissioner of the United States, in and for said district, on the oath of _Sylvester Lewis_ and others, with having

## Sources from the Past

This warrant for Anthony's arrest is a primary source. It states that Anthony is being arrested for voting "without having a lawful right" to vote. After she was found guilty of voting illegally, Anthony was fined $100. She refused to pay the fine, and the government never forced her to pay. What does this warrant tell you about the government's thoughts on the Fourteenth Amendment? How do primary sources help historians understand laws from the past?

23

# RISE OF THE NAWSA

In 1890, the NWSA and the AWSA came together again after 21 years apart. The new organization was called the National American Woman Suffrage Association (NAWSA). Its leaders worked to gain suffrage one state at a time. They hoped Congress would pass an amendment for women's suffrage after a majority of states gave women the right to vote. Carrie Chapman Catt became the NAWSA president in 1900 after Susan B. Anthony stepped down. Catt served until 1904, then again from 1915 until 1920.

SUSAN B. ANTHONY (LEFT) AND ELIZABETH CADY STANTON WORKED TOGETHER FOR OVER 50 YEARS. ANTHONY, STANTON, AND LUCY STONE WERE THE FIRST LEADERS OF THE NAWSA.

Official Program WOMAN SUFFRAGE Procession

VOTES FOR WOMEN

Washington D.C. March 3, 1913

By 1896, Wyoming, Colorado, Utah, and Idaho had gained full suffrage. Between 1910 and 1914, Washington, California, Oregon, Kansas, Arizona, Alaska, Montana, and Nevada also passed full women's suffrage. In 1917, New York became the first state east of the Mississippi River to allow women to vote in all elections.

# THE 1913 WOMAN'S SUFFRAGE PARADE

Alice Paul was the head of the National Woman's Party, another suffragist group. She organized a suffrage march on Washington, D.C., March 3, 1913. More than 5,000 suffragists attended the parade. They marched to get the country's attention about women's suffrage.

White suffragists forced black suffragists to march at the back of the parade. Many black suffragists protested this segregation, including Ida B. Wells. She marched in the white section of the parade with suffragists from Illinois, her own state.

A crowd of angry people who were against women's suffrage interrupted the parade. Army troops were sent in to control the mob, and the suffragists were able to finish their march. This was an important event in the suffrage movement because it brought suffragists from across the country together.

# WOMAN'S JOURNAL
## AND SUFFRAGE NEWS

VOL. XLIV. NO. 10       SATURDAY, MARCH 8, 1913       FIVE CENTS

## PARADE STRUGGLES TO VICTORY DESPITE DISGRACEFUL SCENES

### Nation Aroused by Open Insults to Women—Cause Wins Popular Sympathy—Congress Orders Investigation—Striking Object Lesson

Washington has been disgraced. Equal suffrage has scored a great victory. Thousands of indifferent women have been aroused. Influential men are incensed and the United States Senate demands an investigation of the treatment given the suffragists at the National Capital on Monday.

Ten thousand women from all over the country had planned a magnificent parade and pageant to take place in Washington on March 3. Artists, pageant leaders, designers, women of influence and renown were ready to give a wonderful and beautiful piece of suffrage work to the public that would throng the National Capital for the inauguration festivities. The suffragists asked the police protection, when the police protection, that had been promised, failed them, and a disgraceful scene followed. The crowd surged into the space which had been marked off for the parade, and the leaders of the suffrage movement were compelled to push their way through a mob of the worst element in Washington and vicinity. Women were spit upon, slapped in the face, tripped up, pelted with burning cigar stubs, and insulted by jeers and obscene language too vile to print or repeat.

The cause of all the trouble is apparent when the facts are known. The police authorities in Washington opposed every attempt to have a suffrage parade at all. Having been forbidden a place in the inaugural procession, the suffragists asked to have a procession of their own on March 3. They were finally told that they could have a procession but that it could not be on Pennsylvania Avenue, but must be on a side street. At last they got permission to have the suffrage parade on the avenue, and asked that traffic be excluded from the street during the parade. For a long time this was denied, and only on Saturday were they successful.

Everything was at last arranged; it was a glorious day; ten thousand women were ready to do their part to make the parade beautiful to behold, to make it a credit to womanhood and to demonstrate the strength of the movement for their enfranchisement.

The police were determined, however, and they had their way. Their attempt to afford the marchers protection and keep the space of the avenue free for the suffrage procession was the flimsiest sham. Police officers stood by with folded arms and grinned while the picked women of the land were insulted and roughly abused by an ignorant and uncouth mob.

Miss Alice Paul and other suffragists were compelled to drive their automobiles down the avenue to separate the crowds so the suffragists with the banners and floats could pass. The police officials say their force was inadequate to handle the crowds, but it is noted that there was no disorder on the avenue during the inaugural procession. It is stated that federal troops were offered to the chief of police for the suffrage procession, but that he refused their aid.

At any rate, assistance was finally called from Fort Myer and mounted soldiers drove back the crowd so that a straggling line of marchers could pass through.

Not only were the suffragists bitterly disappointed in having the effect

(Continued on Page 78)

### AMENDMENT WINS IN NEW JERSEY

Easy Victory in Assembly 46 to 5—Equal Suffrage Enthusiasm Runs High

The New Jersey Legislature passed the woman suffrage amendment in the Assembly last week by a vote of 46 to 5. The Senate had already voted favorably 14 to 5.

A large delegation of suffragists crowded the galleries, and when the overwhelming vote was announced there was a scene of great enthusiasm. Women stood in their seats and waved handkerchiefs and "votes for women" flags and cheered themselves hoarse.

**Dr. Jekyll Becomes Mr. Hyde**

(Continued on Page 79)

### MICHIGAN AGAIN CAMPAIGN STATE

Senate Passes Suffrage Amendment 26 to 5 and Battle Is Now On

Michigan is again a campaign State after a short lapse of four months. The amendment will go to the voters on April 7. The State-wide feeling that the women were defrauded of victory last fall will help the suffragists.

The final action of the Legislature was taken last week, when the Senate, by a vote of 26 to 5, passed the suffrage amendment, with a slight amendment to make the requirements for foreign-born women the same as those for main line women.

**Congress Watches Debate**

The debate in the Senate lasted an hour and a quarter, and was characterized by the persistent efforts of Senator Wenlock and a few others to tack on crippling amendments. Several suggestions, including the disabling of women for holding office or serving on juries, were voted down in quick succession.

Gov. Ferris was among the visitors who crowded the chamber and gallery. Mrs. Utica B. Arthur, Mrs. Thomas R. Henderson and Mrs. Wilbur Brotherton, of Detroit; Mrs. Jennie Law Hardy, of Tecumseh, and other State leaders were present, supported by a large delegation of Lansing suffragists.

The final stand of the opposition was made by Senator Murtha in the hope of putting off the submission till November, 1914, and this also failed. Of the five who opposed the measure on the final roll-call, three were from Detroit.

A complete campaign of organization and education has been mapped out by the State Association. The

(Continued on Page 74)

General Rosalie Jones in Pilgrim Costume; Miss Inez Milholland on White Steed Leading the Parade; One of the Scores of Imposing Floats; One View of the Procession

---

## Sources from the Past

Articles in newspapers are primary sources when they report on recent events. The article about the 1913 suffrage parade in this issue of *Woman's Journal* is a primary source. It was published shortly after the parade took place. The article talks about how the mob yelled at and hurt the women marching. What does this primary source tell you about society's thoughts on women's rights in the early 1900s?

# THE NINETEENTH AMENDMENT

Alice Paul and the National Woman's Party protested outside the White House to get President Woodrow Wilson's support for women's suffrage. President Wilson agreed to support women's suffrage in 1918. Finally, on June 4, 1919, both the House of Representatives and the Senate agreed to pass the Nineteenth Amendment, also known as the Susan B. Anthony Amendment.

Suffragists worked to get the amendment ratified, or formally approved, by 36 states so it would become part of the Constitution. Their final campaign lasted another 14 months. In February of 1920, the NAWSA changed its name to the League of Women Voters.

On August 18, 1920, the Nineteenth Amendment to the Constitution was passed. More than 72 years after the Seneca Falls Convention, women finally had the right to vote in all U.S. elections.

ALICE PAUL USED STRONGER FORMS OF PROTEST THAN MANY SUFFRAGISTS. SHE LED HUNGER STRIKES, WHICH MEANT SHE AND HER FOLLOWERS REFUSED TO EAT IN ORDER TO RAISE AWARENESS OF WOMEN'S SUFFRAGE.

# WOMEN'S RIGHTS TODAY

Earning the right to vote finally gave women a voice in government. Winning suffrage wasn't the end of the women's rights movement, though. Women still weren't treated equally, especially in the workplace. The Civil Rights Act of 1964 made it illegal to discriminate against people because of their race, religion, national origin, or gender. This important law protected women alongside black Americans and other **minorities**.

Even a century after the Nineteenth Amendment passed, women aren't treated equal to men in all ways. The Women's March of 2017 showed that women in the United States and around the world are still fighting for equal rights today. This time, activists marched for many issues, including women's rights, racial equality, and rights for minority groups.

# GLOSSARY

**activist:** Someone who acts strongly in support of or against an issue.

**convention:** A gathering of people who have a common interest.

**discriminate:** To treat people unequally based on class, race, religion, or gender.

**gender:** The state of being male or female.

**lynch:** To kill someone, usually by hanging, through mob action and without legal permission.

**minority:** A group of people who are different from the larger group in a country or other area in some way, such as race or religion.

**pamphlet:** A short printed publication with no cover or with a paper cover.

**petition:** A formal written request to a leader or government regarding a particular cause.

**racist:** Someone who believes that one group or race of people is better than another group or race.

**registration:** The act or process of entering information about something or someone into a book or system of public records.

**segregate:** To separate people based on race, class, or ethnicity.

**violence:** Using force to harm someone.

**warrant:** A document issued by a legal or government official giving a police officer permission to take action to carry out the law.

# INDEX

# WEBSITES

Due to the changing nature of Internet links, PowerKids Press has developed an online list of websites related to the subject of this book. This site is updated regularly. Please use this link to access the list: www.powerkidslinks.com/eohs/suffrage